MW00899065

TELL ME A STORY

DOVER PUBLICATIONS, INC.
MINEOLA, NEW YORK

education.com

Copyright

Copyright © 2010, 2011, 2012, 2013, 2014, 2015 by Education.com
All rights reserved.

Bibliographical Note

Tell Me a Story, first published by Dover Publications, Inc., in 2015, contains
pages from the following online workbooks published by Education.com:
Read Between the Lines; A Feast of Fairy Tales; Make Believe and *The Three Billy
Goats Gruff;* and *Jack and the Beanstalk.*

International Standard Book Number

ISBN-13: 978-0-486-80258-9
ISBN-10: 0-486-80258-2

Manufactured in the United States by Courier Corporation
80258201   2015
www.doverpublications.com

CONTENTS

READ
BETWEEN
THE LINES

MAKING INFERENCES

Introduction

Answers aren't always right or wrong in this series. It's all about thinking things through and exercising reasoning skills. This workbook is about storytelling and filling in the gaps!

Read passages aloud with your child and have him practice his reading.

As you go through the Making Inferences and Cause & Effect pages with your child, help explore why he, or she, came to the conclusions that he did.

MAKING INFERENCES

What is happening in each picture? Circle your best guess.

The chef is happily cooking a spaghetti dinner.

The chef is preparing breakfast for his family.

The plane is taking off from the airport.

The plane is landing after a 14 hour flight.

The fisherwoman returned the fish to the sea.

The fisherwoman caught a fish for dinner.

The man dug up an old tree.

The man planted a beautiful new tree.

The bird returned to his nest with food.

The bird is preparing to fly and go find food.

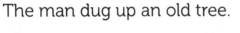

 TREASURE HUNT

Arrrggghhh, matey! Can you piece together these pictures from beginning to end to show the pirates discovering a great treasure?

Write each phrase below onto the appropriate picture.

Land, ho!

Success!

Unload the supplies

X marks the spot

CAUSE & EFFECT

A cause is the reason why something happens. An effect is what happens.

Cause
Because Rachel studied,

Effect
she got an A on her test.

Circle the best way to end each sentence.

Kevin has a fever

because he played in the rain.

because he stayed home yesterday.

The cat is happy

because she is going to eat.

because she is going to the doctor.

Because the team won the game,

the fan was hungry.

the fan was happy.

The family ordered a large pizza

because they forgot to make dinner.

because they were full.

Because the flowers were not watered,

they were strong and healthy.

they were dry and weak.

Because Joe always brushed his teeth,

he had to see the dentist often.

he never had a cavity.

The man went for a bike ride because

the weather was good.

he was tired.

CAUSE & EFFECT

Read the stories. Underline each sentence that tells why something happened.

1.) Sammy's mother told her that dinner was almost ready. Sammy was very hungry and decided to eat some sweets before dinner. When dinner was ready, Sammy was feeling too sick to eat.

Why didn't Sammy eat dinner?

She didn't like what her mom cooked.

She ordered a pizza instead.

She felt sick after eating sweets.

2.) Ben went out for a quick bike ride. Since he wasn't going too far, he decided not to check his tires. As he was getting close to home his front tire went flat. He checked to see if he ran over a nail, but did not see any damage.

Why did the front tire go flat?

It was a cheap tire.

Ben forgot to check it before he left.

The tire was too hot.

3.) Walter waters his lawn every week. His kids like to play on the fresh grass. He also puts fertilizer on the grass to make sure it stays healthy. If he forgets to water the lawn, the grass and bushes would become unhealthy and dry.

What keeps Walter's lawn healthy?

His kids playing on it

Forgetting to water it

Watering and fertilizing it

4.) Benny the cat was sleeping soundly at home. Suddenly, a little mouse squeaked by him. Even though he was tired, Benny the cat opened his eyes.

Why did Benny the cat wake up?

He was late for an appointment.

He was hungry.

A mouse squeaked by.

MAKING INFERENCES

Look at each set of pictures and try to figure out what happened. Circle your answer.

The baseball broke the window.

- - - - - - - - - - - - - - - - - -

The man stole the ball from the kid.

- - - - - - - - - - - - - - - - - -

The man found his old baseball.

The policeman crashed his patrol car.

- - - - - - - - - - - - - - - - - -

The red car was speeding.

- - - - - - - - - - - - - - - - - -

The red car ran out of gas.

The girl baked a tasty chocolate cake.

- - - - - - - - - - - - - - - - - -

The girl bought a chocolate cake.

- - - - - - - - - - - - - - - - - -

The girl cooked dinner.

8

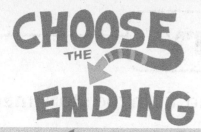

CHOOSE THE ENDING

Read each story beginning. Then, circle the sentence ending that makes the most sense.

Ben was walking home from school when he found a wallet full of money. His parents had always taught him to be honest. Ben picked up the wallet and...

- kept on walking.
- tried to find the owner.

Sammy woke up to a giant snow storm. She checked the temperature gauge on the wall and it was 10 degrees Fahrenheit. Sammy decided to wear...

- her heavy coat and boots.
- a light jacket and sneakers.

Chris has been practicing all year for the big game. His pitching has really improved over the season. On the first pitch of the game, he...

- threw a nice curveball.
- kicked the ball to the batter.

Map the Story

Read the story below. Using what you've read, fill in the **story map**.

Mila wanted to ride her bike. Her mother told her to put on her knee pads. Mila didn't like to wear knee pads, so she didn't put them on. While riding down the sidewalk, Mila fell off of her bike and scraped her knee. She went home and apologized to her mom, promising to wear her pads from now on.

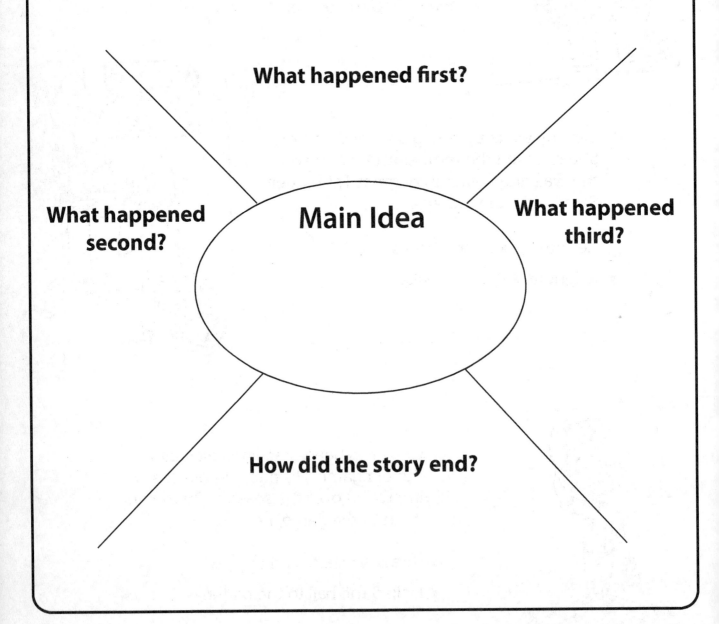

What happened first?

What happened second?

Main Idea

What happened third?

How did the story end?

MAP THE STORY

Read the story below. Using what you've read, fill in the story map.

"Mary was excited! Today was the day of her tea party lunch! She had invited three friends to join her for tea and sandwiches, so she knew she had to get busy in the kitchen before her guests arrived. Mary decided to make her favorite lunch... peanut butter and jelly sandwiches! First, she spread peanut butter on four slices of bread. Next, Mary began to spread grape jelly (her favorite) onto the peanut butter. Then she remembered that two of her friends did not like grape jelly. Quickly, she found the strawberry jam in the cupboard and spread it on to the last two peanut butter slices. Mary covered each sandwich with a second slice of bread and then cut each sandwich in half. She placed them on a tray right next to her beautiful china teapot. Suddenly the doorbell rang... Mary's tea party guests had arrived, and just in time for lunch!"

What did Mary do first?

Finally, what did Mary do last?

What did Mary do next?

Main Idea

Then what did Mary do?

Beginning

DRAW THE STORY

It's time to set your imagination free and complete the story below. How did the story begin? What will the ending be? It's all up to you, so take out your favorite drawing supplies and have fun!

Middle

Middle

Middle

End

FILL IN THE STORY

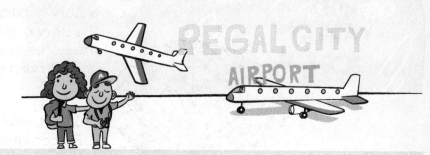

Complete the story by writing in the empty boxes below.

BEGINNING

Sara and her brother Kevin were getting ready to fly to Texas to visit their grandparents. This would be the first time either of them flew without their mom or dad.
Before they left, Sara's mom said, "Make sure to look after your brother and your bags!"

MIDDLE 1

After they reached their gate, Sara's brother said he was hungry. Since there was still a lot of time left before their flight left, Sara took her brother to get something to eat.

MIDDLE 3

Their plane was getting ready to take off, and they still had not found their missing bags!

MIDDLE 2

END

FIND THE MAIN IDEA

The **main idea** is the most important idea of a story or paragraph. The main idea tells what the story or paragraph is mostly about. Read the stories below carefully and circle the correct main idea of each.

Susie threw the Frisbee for Pete. The Frisbee landed in a tall tree. It was stuck in the branches. Pete barked and barked. Then a gust of wind blew the Frisbee loose. Pete finally caught the Frisbee. He stopped barking and started wagging his tail instead.

What is the main idea?

1. Pete barks at squirrels in the tree
2. Pete is excited to play fetch with his toy.

The three little birds patiently waited for their mom to return with lunch. Their stomachs grumbled as they thought about their favorite food: worms! It was a windy day so it took their mom longer to return. They played a game to keep their minds off of lunch. When their mom returned, they quickly ate up the worms.

What is the main idea?

1. The little birds were very hungry.
2. It was a windy day.

Scott was having a very busy day. He needed to write a report, answer the phone and check his email. His boss came by and dropped off some papers. At noon, he quickly ate his lunch. When he returned to his desk he checked his messages and got back to work.

What is the main idea?

1. Scott ate his lunch after work.
2. Scott is having a very busy day at work.

Find The Main Idea

The **_main idea_** is the most important idea in a paragraph. Sometimes, the main idea is the first sentence. Sometimes the main idea is in the middle or at the end. Read the paragraphs carefully. Circle the main idea.

Kittens need special care. You have to feed kittens twice a day. They have a lot of energy. You need to play with them often. Kittens will chew on almost anything they find. You have to watch them closely.

What is the main idea?

1. Kittens will chew on almost anything.

2. Kittens need special care.

The puppy began to eat, but then he stopped. He yawned and stretched. He chased his tail. He rolled over and barked. He licked his paw. Finally, he went back to his dish and finished eating.

What is the main idea?

1. The puppy likes to eat.

2. The puppy takes a long time to eat.

15

What Happens Next?

Read the story. Decide what might happen next.

Adi's mom asks Adi not to open the window. If he does, bugs might fly into the house. It's very hot inside. Adi opens the window just a little. Then sees a butterfly flying toward the window.

Draw a picture of what you think will happen next.

———

Write what you think will happen next.

And Then What Happened?

Read the story and predict what happens next!

It was a beautiful spring morning and Priscilla the bear decided to take a walk through the woods. She was enjoying the sunshine and smelling the flowers when she suddenly heard somebody crying. Priscilla looked around to see who was crying. She spotted a baby bird sitting on the ground next to a tree. She asked, "Why are you crying?" The baby bird replied, "I fell out of my nest and I can't get back up the tree." Priscilla looked up at the bird's nest in the tree and said, "I can help you, little bird."

What do you think happened next? Write the end of the story here.

_____

_____

_____

_____

_____

_____

What do you think Priscilla was thinking when she heard the baby bird crying?

_____

_____

How do you think the baby bird felt when he fell out of the nest?

_____

_____

17

AND THEN WHAT HAPPENED?

Read the story and predict what happens next!

A space mission from Earth landed on a faraway planet named Bogo. As the astronaut began exploring the rocky planet, he heard what sounded like two people talking. Confused, he walked closer to the source of the noise. It seemed like the conversation was coming from behind a giant rock. He picked up the large rock an was amazed at what he saw: two little green aliens!

What do you think happened next? Write the end of the story here.

_____

_____

_____

_____

_____

Who do you think was more surprised, the astronaut or the aliens?

_____

_____

What do you think the two aliens were talking about before they were discovered?

_____

_____

What would you do if you were the astronaut?

_____

_____

_____

WHAT HAPPENS NEXT?

Ben's parents bought him a new football for his birthday. His mom warned him not to throw the ball inside the house. When Ben's friend came over to watch a football game, they couldn't resist testing out the new football. As Ben threw the ball to his friend, he realized it was heading straight towards his mother's favorite vase!

Draw a picture of what you think will happen next.

Write what you think will happen next.

READING COMPREHENSION PRACTICE

Read the paragraphs. Draw a circle around the correct answer to each question.

My family went to the first baseball game of the season. We sat near the field and the action was very close. Suddenly, the ball came towards us. Luckily, my sister and I brought our gloves.

What most likely happened next?

They caught the ball.

The ballgame ended.

They went to go buy popcorn.

Rob loves his dog Dougie very much. Every morning he fills up his food bowl. Then he gives him a bath. In the afternoon, he takes Dougie for a walk in the park. Dougie is a very happy and well-loved dog!

What is the first thing Rob does for his dog every morning?

He walks Dougie.

He buys him treats.

He fills up his food bowl.

The countryside is very calm. The water flows gently. Birds happily chirp as the calm breeze cools the air. A man quietly naps in his row boat.

What is the main idea?

The countryside is crowded

The countryside is peaceful.

The man is lazy.

20

Great job!

is an Education.com reading superstar

A FEAST OF FAIRY TALES

FAIRY TALE ORGANIZER

All stories are different, but every story has important details like characters, setting, and plot. Use this graphic organizer to show the important details of your favorite fairy tale.

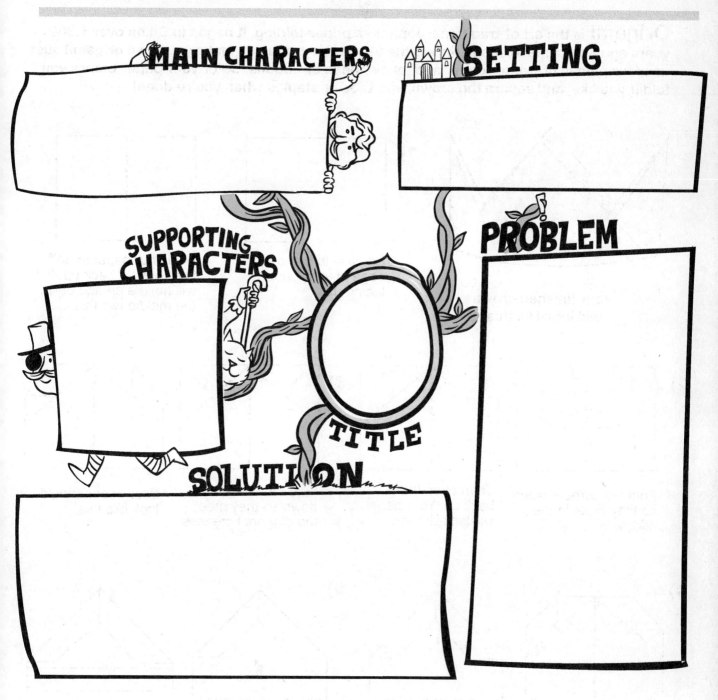

MAIN CHARACTERS

SETTING

SUPPORTING CHARACTERS

PROBLEM

TITLE

SOLUTION

Learn to fold *Origami!*

Origami is the art of traditional Japanese paper-folding. It began in China over 1,800 years ago and came to Japan during the 6th century. You can make your own origami! Just use four pieces of printer paper and follow these directions. Color your paper before you fold if you like, and secure the crown with tape or staples when you're done!

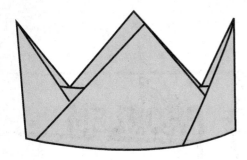

Your finished crown will look like this!

1)

Begin with the longer edge of your paper facing up.

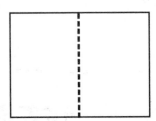

Fold your paper in half, then open it back up. It will have a crease down the middle like this.

2)

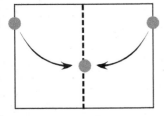

Fold the corners down so they meet in the middle.

Then open them back up. Your paper will look like this.

3)

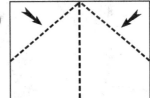

Fold the corners down so they meet the diagonal creases.

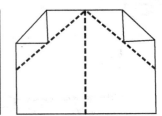

Your paper should look like this.

4)

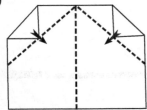

Fold the diagonal creases back over.

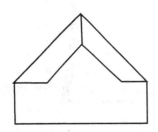

Your paper will look like this.

5)

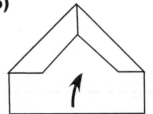

Fold the bottom of the paper up to meet the flat parts in the triangle.

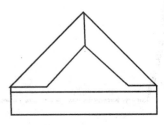

Your paper will look like this.

5)

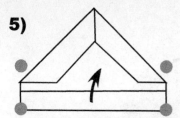

Fold the bottom up again, so it creases along the base of the triangle.

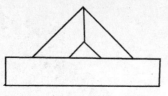

Your paper will look like this.

6)

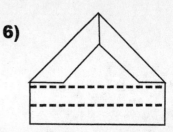

Unfold the bottom so your paper looks like this. Then, follow steps 1 - 5 with three more pieces of paper.

6)

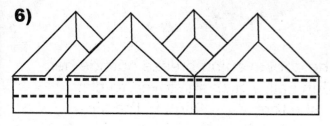

Arrange the four pieces so they overlap as shown here.

7)

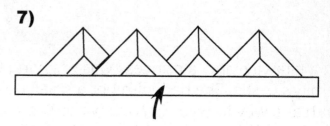

Fold up at the first crease, then at the second, joining the row of triangles like this.

8)

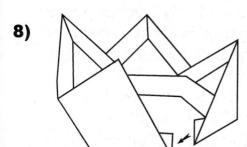

Bend the line into a circle. Tuck one end of the strip into the other.

9)

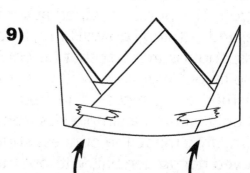

Tape or staple the four pieces together.

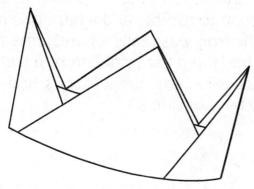

Your crown is complete! Put it on your head and enjoy being royalty!

THE FROG PRINCE

In a faraway land, a princess was enjoying the cool evening breeze outside her family's castle. She had with her a small golden ball, which she loved to play with as a way to relax. On one particular toss, she threw it so high in the air that she lost track of it, and the ball went rolling towards a spring. The ball plopped into the water and quickly sank out of sight. The princess began sobbing in despair, and wished for her toy to return to her.

Then, a small frog popped out from the spring. "What's wrong beautiful princess?" asked the frog. The princess wiped away her tears and said, "My favorite golden ball is gone, and nothing I do will bring it back." The frog tried his best to comfort the princess, and assured her that he could retrieve the ball if she would grant him just one favor. "Anything! I will give you all my jewels and handfuls of gold!" exclaimed the princess. The frog explained that he had no need for riches, and only wanted a simple kiss from her in return. The thought of kissing a slimy frog made the princess shudder, but in the end she agreed, as she really loved her golden ball. Without much effort, the agile frog jumped back into the spring and located the golden ball. In a blink of an eye the frog had retrieved the ball and returned it to the princess. Keeping her word, the princess kissed the frog. Suddenly, the ground began to rumble and a haze of smoke filled the air. To the princess's surprise, the frog was really a handsome prince trapped by an evil witch's curse. Her kiss had freed the prince from a lifetime of pain and misery. The prince and princess became great friends, and eventually wed in a beautiful ceremony by the spring.

The Frog Prince
Fairytale storyboard

Oh no! This story has gotten all mixed up. Can you put the scenes from this famous fairytale in the right order?

Bonus activity: Color in the scenes with your favorite colors!

cut and reorder

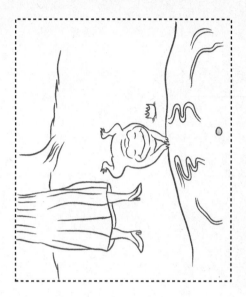

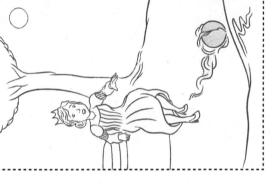

THE PRINCESS AND THE PEA!

Once upon a time there was a prince looking to marry a princess. One day, his father and mother asked all the princesses in the area to come over to their castle. Unfortunately, the prince did not get along with any of them. The angry princesses stormed off into the rainy night.

Suddenly, there was a knock at the castle door. The prince opened the door and was surprised to see a beautiful princess standing in the rain. Despite not looking like a princess, with her clothes being soaked and her hair all wet, the prince invited her in from the cold. She told the prince and his family that she was a princess.

The queen was doubtful, and knew of a way to find out if she really was a princess. As the queen prepared the bed for their visitor, she placed a tiny pea under 20 mattresses. Only a true princess would be able to feel the pea! When the princess awoke the next morning, she had a terrible pain in her back. When the prince and his family heard of this, they knew she was indeed a real princess. The prince had found the princess of his dreams, and the two soon got married.

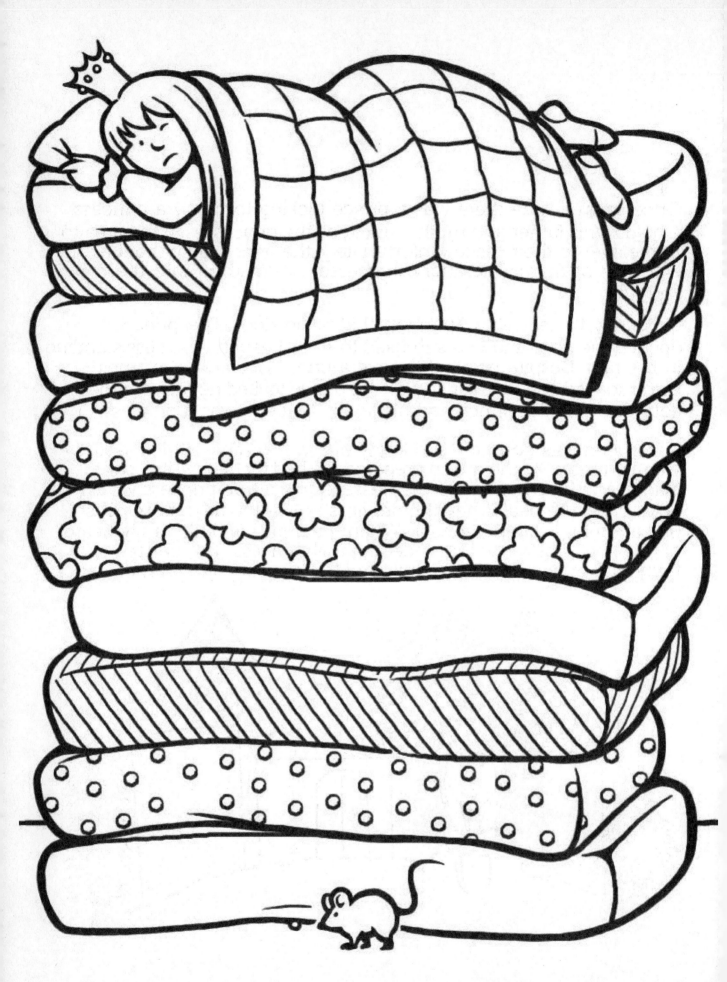

THE PRINCESS AND THE PEA

Oh no, the story has been all jumbled up. It's up to you to cut out the images and make the story make sense again.

Bonus Activity: Color in the images with your favorite colors.

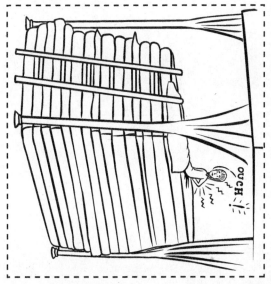

STONE SOUP

One day, in a small village next to a flowing river, two hungry wanderers showed up looking for ingredients to make a delicious soup. Since the two had no money, none of the villagers were willing to give them any vegetables or meat. With no ingredients, the two went down to the river and filled their pot with water. They then placed a large stone in the pot and began boiling their soup. Soon, a curious villager asked them what they were doing. One of the men answered, "We are cooking Stone Soup, but we are still missing a few ingredients to finish it properly." The villager said she did not mind giving them some ingredients, if she could have some as well. The two men said they would be happy to share with the entire village once the soup was ready. After the word spread, many villagers brought spices, vegetables, and meat to add to the soup. In the end, everyone enjoyed the hearty soup!

STONE SOUP

Oh no, the story has been all jumbled up. It's up to you to cut out the images and make the story make sense again.

Bonus Activity: Color in the images with your favorite colors.

RUMPELSTILTSKIN

Once upon a time, there was an old carpenter who wanted to impress the king. Since he did not have great wealth, he told the king that his daughter could spin straw into gold. After hearing this, the king quickly called for the daughter and locked her into a room full of straw. "Turn this straw into gold, or I will leave you in this room forever," said the king. The carpenter's daughter did not know what to do! She did not know how to spin straw into gold.

As she cried, a small and ugly creature appeared, and asked her why she was crying. "If I don't turn this straw into gold, I will be locked in this room forever," wept the girl. The creature said he could spin the straw into gold, but wanted her necklace in return. She agreed, and the creature magically spun all of the straw into solid gold coins.

The next day, the king was overjoyed to find the room full of gold. He moved the girl into an even larger room, filled with more straw. "Turn all this straw into gold, or I will lock you in this room forever!" said the king.

The strange creature appeared the next night to work his magic again. This time, he wanted the young woman's ring. She gave the creature her ring, and once again he spun all of the straw in the room into gold. When the king walked into the room the next morning, the gold was at eye level. Ecstatic, the king moved the girl into yet an even larger room. This time however, he told the carpenter's daughter that he would marry her if she succeeded one last time.

Like the nights before, the creature appeared again and offered his help. With no more jewelery to take, the creature demanded the young woman's first-born child instead. She reluctantly agreed, and once again the creature turned the straw into gold. The king promptly married the carpenter's daughter, and they eventually had a beautiful little baby. On one stormy night, the creature returned to claim the young woman's first born child. She did not want to give up her precious baby, and offered the creature jewels and riches instead. He refused her offer, but instead told her, "If you can guess my name, I will disappear forever. I'll give you one week to think!" Smartly, the young woman sent a messenger to follow the creature to his home. From behind the trees, he overheard the creature singing a song which revealed his name. The messenger rushed back to tell the young woman the good news. When the creature returned one week later, the carpenter's daughter screamed out, "Rumpelstiltskin", and in a puff of smoke, the creature disappeared forever.

RUMPELSTILTSKIN

Oh no, the story has been all jumbled up. It's up to you to cut out the images and make the story make sense again.

Bonus Activity: Color in the images with your favorite colors.

THE UGLY DUCKLING

It was a beautiful spring morning on a small farm near the woods. In a cool, shaded corner, a duck built a warm nest to sit on her four precious eggs. Strangely, one of the eggs was much larger than the rest. To her excitement, the eggs started to rumble and crack. One, two, three eggs popped open, and three little ducklings poked their heads into the world. At the same time, the oddly large egg began to crack as well. To the mother's surprise, a big gray duckling stumbled out of the egg. Although he was different, and not as cute as the other ducklings, she loved him nonetheless. The next day, the duck introduced her family to the other animals on the farm. Seeing the strange gray duckling, the pig, duck and mouse burst out laughing.

The poor duckling bowed his head in shame as he felt he didn't belong. That night, as his family slept near the barn, the gray duckling decided to leave on a journey to find himself. Before long, he ran into a kind old woman, her rooster, and her cat. She invited him into her home, and they all treated him like family. Over the year, the little gray duckling began to grow. Although he was happy, he always felt something was missing. One day, as he stared out on the pond, he saw a family of beautiful swans wading in the cool breeze. Something inside him wanted to go swimming with the swans. As he approached the pond, he saw his reflection for the first time. The ugly gray duckling had grown into a beautiful swan! From below, the cat and rooster happily watch their friend fly high in the sky. Finally, the little gray duckling had found himself.

THE UGLY DUCKLING

Oh no, the story has been all jumbled up. It's up to you to cut out the images and make the story make sense again.

Bonus Activity: Color in the images with your favorite colors.

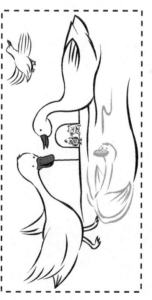

 # Make Your Own Fairy Tale

Fairy tales offer readers fun, adventurous stories full of talking animals, candy-covered houses and transformation, not to mention princes and princesses. Explore your child's favorite fairy tale with her, and learn about characters, plot, setting and story sequence while she draws her own pictures.

What You Need:

- Paper
- Crayons

What You Do:

1. Encourage your child to tell you her favorite fairy tale. Don't correct her if she gets some of the details wrong. Let this be her version. As she tells the story, ask her how she would draw various scenes or details. If the story is "Goldilocks and the Three Bears", how do you show porridge is hot, or cold, or just right?

2. When she is done telling the story, give her the paper and crayons and encourage her to draw something that you talked about. Is this enough for someone else to know the story? Probably not, so help her fill in the details.

3. Start with the characters. Who is this story about? Who is the "good guy," or hero, and who is the "bad guy," or villain? Draw your own pictures while she draws her version.

4. Where does this story take place? Encourage her to draw a scene that shows the setting – Goldilocks peeking into the bear's house or Jack climbing up the beanstalk.

5. As she draws, lay the pictures out in the order they occur in the story. While she's developing this sequence, she'll see that pieces are still missing. Time for more drawing!

6. After your child has completed her drawings, bind them together in a notebook or simply staple them together.

Start a fairy tale library of stories retold and illustrated by members of your family. Draw each other's favorites to compare and contrast your versions of each tale. After everyone has done their favorite stories, you can explore other fairy tales at the library.

Great job!

is an Education.com reading superstar

MAKE BELIEVE AND
THE THREE
BILLY GOATS GRUFF

The Three Billy Goats Gruff
mini book

How to Make the Mini Book

What You Need:
The story pages
Paste or a glue stick

1. Tear out the story pages and fold each in half on the dotted line.
2. Fold page one so that the image is on the outside. This will be the book cover.
3. Fold page two the opposite way of page one, so that the image and text face each other.
4. You'll want to fold the rest of the pages the same as page two.
5. Time to glue! Take page two and page three and put a thin layer of paste on the backsides of the paper. Make sure to get the edge.

Put glue
here and here.

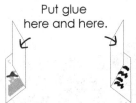

6. Line up the papers corner to corner and press the two halves together.

Your finished book should look something like this
with all of the pages glued to each other.

The Three Billy Goats Gruff

Once upon a time there were three billy goats, all named Gruff.

Goats eat a lot, you know, and one day they found that their grassy hill was becoming bare. There was more grass to eat on the other side of the river.

The smallest Gruff decided to go first. To get there he had to cross a bridge. Under the bridge lived a great big troll.

Trip, trap, trip, trap, trip, trap went the bridge.

"Who comes crossing my bridge?" said the troll.

"It is only I, Little Billy Goat Gruff," said the billy goat, with a tiny voice.

"I will eat you up!" said the troll.

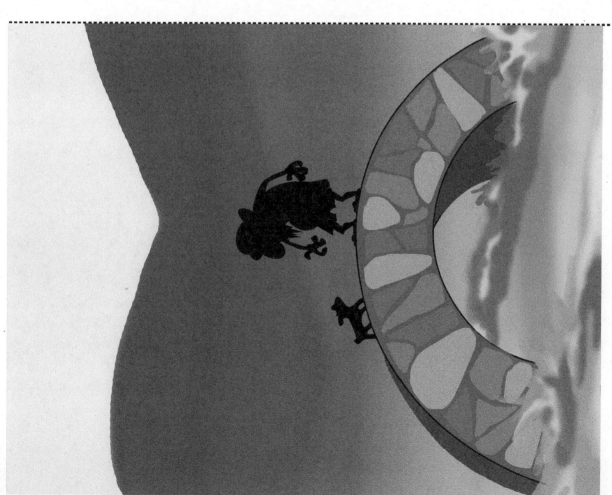

"Oh you do not want to do that. I am too little," said the billy goat. "Wait, and my big brother will come along. He's bigger than me. He will make a much better meal."

"Be gone then! I will wait for a bigger, better meal," said the troll.

And with that the little billy goat quickly crossed to the other side.

After a little while the bridge shook.

Trip, trap, trip, trap, trip, trap.

"Who comes crossing my bridge?"
yelled the troll.

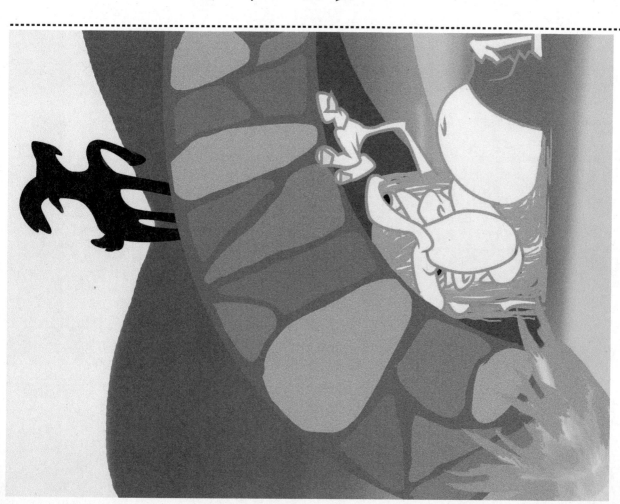

"It is I, Medium Billy Goat Gruff."

"I will eat you up!" cried the troll, coming closer.

"If you wait just a little my big brother will come along. Don't eat me. He is much bigger."

"Be gone then," said the troll.

And then TRIP, TRAP, TRIP, TRIP, TRAP, TRIP, TRAP. The bridge groaned uner a very heavy goat.

"Now who comes crossing my bridge?" demanded the troll, now very angry indeed.

"It is I! Big Billy Goat Gruff."

"Now I'm coming to gobble you up!" yelled the troll.

"Well, come along," said the biggest billy goat Gruff.

The troll ran at him. Big Gruff thumped the troll hard in the chest with his big horns.

The troll went right off the bridge and into the water, where he hurt his foot. He had wanted the biggest mouthful for himself and ended up all wet instead.

The three billy goats had their fill of grass from the hills on that side of the river.

The End

The Three Billy Goats Gruff

Ideas for writing and storytelling practice

With 10 coloring page scenes kids can use these writing pages to:

 Practice story sequencing by putting the scenes in the order that the story happened.

 Use the pages out of order to create their own version of The Three Billy Goats Gruff.

 Make up an all new story!

 Use them as drawing pages to draw new items into each scene, or change the weather or time of day.

 Use as graphic organizers or note taking paper for researching facts about real goats (like fainting goats, mountain goats or how about that herd that scaled a dam in Italy!)

Each character of the story is featured on his own page. These can be used to:

 Describe how each character sounds and smells.

 Make a character profile by answering questions about each character like how old they are, what they like to eat for breakfast, where they last went.

 Write about the experience of crossing the bridge from each character's perspective.

 As story starters for separate stories for each character...
- o   What was Big Gruff like when he was younger?
- o   Imagine what the troll's happiest day ever was.
- o   What did each character do after the bridge was crossed?

77

The Three Billy Goats Gruff: Make Masks

Who's that tripping over my bridge? Trick the troll with an easy-to-make goat mask perfect for acting out the tale of the Three Billy Goats Gruff. Not only will your child have a new prop for dramatic play, he'll also get to work on his fine motor skills. This fun craft will have your child over the bridge and out of harm's way in no time.

What You Need:

5 paper plates
Cotton balls
Black marker
Pink marker
Scissors
Glue
Elastic string
Hole punch

What You Do:

1. Have your child use the scissors to cut off the outer rim of one of the paper plates.
2. Show him how to fold the rim in half and cut out two horns for the goat.
3. Fold the remaining center of the plate in half and cut out two almond-shaped ears.
4. Take another one of the plates and turn it over. Give the goat a face by drawing eyes, a nose, and a mouth with the black marker. You may want to provide your child with a model if he seems stumped.
5. Tease apart several cotton balls so that they resemble a wispy goat beard.
6. Ask your child to glue the cotton balls to the goat's chin.
7. Glue the goat's horns to the outer rim of the plate.
8. Using the pink marker, have your child add a little detail to the ears.
9. Ask your child to position and glue the ears to the plate.
10. Create two holes with the scissors near the goat's eyes so that your child will be able to see where he's going.
11. Use the hole punch to punch a hole on each side of the plate.
12. Measure, cut, and attach a piece of elastic cord so that the mask will stay put on your child's head.

After you're done making one mask, encourage your child to make two more so that he has one for each of the three billy goats gruff.

Great job!

_____

is an Education.com reading superstar

JACK AND
THE BEANSTALK

Jack and the Beanstalk

Follow Along and Count

While reading Jack and the Beanstalk, use this worksheet with a helper to keep track of what Jack carries down the beanstalk.

1. What did Jack carry down the beanstalk?

_____

2. How many?

_____

3. What will Jack use the item(s) for?

_____

_____

_____

Draw a picture of the item(s)

---

1. What did Jack carry down the beanstalk?

_____

2. How many?

_____

3. What will Jack use the item(s) for?

_____

_____

_____

Draw a picture of the item(s)

---

1. What did Jack carry down the beanstalk?

_____

2. How many?

_____

3. What will Jack use the item(s) for?

_____

_____

_____

Draw a picture of the item(s)

89

Jack and the Beanstalk
Story Map

While or after reading Jack and the Beanstalk, organize information about the story in this story map.

Characters

Setting

First

Then

Then

Then

Finally

Once upon a time, a poor young man named Jack lived with his mother on a farm in England. The only money they made was by selling milk from their cow. But the cow was getting older, making less and less milk.

One day, Jack was on his way to the city to sell milk when a stranger offered him a handful of magic beans in exchange for the cow. Jack couldn't resist the idea of owning something magical. He made the trade.

When he got home, his mother was angry. "What were you thinking?" she said. "We need money to buy a new cow, but now all we have are five measly beans!" And she threw the beans out the window.

Jack felt sad. But when he woke up the next morning, they saw that the beans had sprouted into a huge, glittering beanstalk that reached all the way up to the sky! Jack decided to climb to the top to see what was up there.

When he got to the top, Jack couldn't believe his eyes - everything in the house was huge! Suddenly a booming voice startled him. "Fee Fi Fo Fum, I smell the blood of an Englishman!" It was a giant!

"Quick, over here," said another voice. Jack saw a giant old woman standing in the huge kitchen. "We must hide you before my husband sees you, or he'll eat you up!" The Giant's wife picked Jack up and put him in the tea kettle.

"Fee Fi Fo Fum!" roared the Giant as he stepped into the giant kitchen. He began to sniff around, hungry for a snack. "I smell something delicious," he said.

"Nonsense," said the Giant's wife. "Go outside and count your gold coins."
The Giant turned and went outside. Jack waited until nighttime to make his
escape down the beanstalk. But before he left, he took a few gold coins
to help feed his family.

When Jack returned to show his mother the gold coins, she sighed. "This isn't enough to buy a new cow. Go back and see if they have anything else."

Jack climbed back up the beanstalk to the castle. He crept quietly into the kitchen and hid. "Fee Fi Fo Fum! I smell the blood of an Englishman!" bellowed the Giant.

"Don't be silly," said his wife, unaware of Jack's presence. "There's nothing to smell but this magical hen I've got for dinner!" Jack spied a hen on the table, crouched over a nest full of golden eggs.

Jack felt sorry for the hen. When the Giant and his wife were busy setting the table, Jack picked up the magical hen and ran. The Giant heard the noise and saw Jack fleeing out the door. "Stop, thief!" he cried, but it was too late.

Jack climbed down the beanstalk and handed his mother the hen. They made a nest for her out of straw. Just then the hen laid a gleaming, golden egg. His mother was shocked. "They must have endless amounts of gold up there!" she laughed.

He quietly crept into the castle once again. This time he heard music and followed it into a hall. Jack saw the Giant strumming a delicate golden harp that could sing by itself! As the Giant fell asleep to the melody, Jack snuck into the room, grabbed the harp, and ran for the door.

As Jack ran, the harp cried for help! "Fee Fi Fo Fum!" the Giant roared. Jack rushed out with the harp under his arm and scurried down the beanstalk. But this time, the Giant followed him!

Jack shouted as loudly as he could. "Mother! Bring me an axe, quickly!"
His mother fetched the axe from the chopping block and met him with it.
Jack began chopping the base of the beanstalk until it split in two. The
beanstalk and the giant disappeared.

Jack and his mother lived happily ever after. And as for the Giant, he is still roaming around in the clouds, searching for a way back up to his castle.

Jack and the Beanstalk

Measuring Beanstalks

More magic beans have sprouted!
**Cut the ruler out below or use a ruler
from home to measure each beanstalk.**

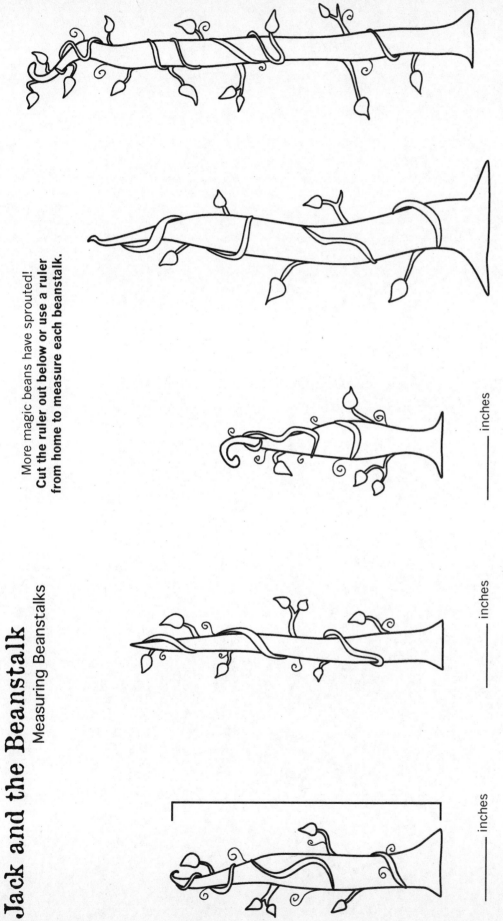

—— inches

—— inches

—— inches

—— inches

—— inches

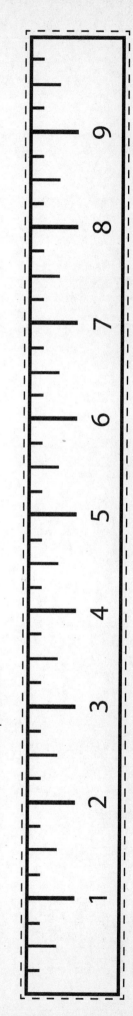

Cut ruler out as close to dotted lines as possible.

Jack and the Beanstalk
Measuring the Climb

It looks like Jack and his friends are climbing the beanstalks. **Cut the ruler out below or use a ruler from home to measure how far each character has climbed.**

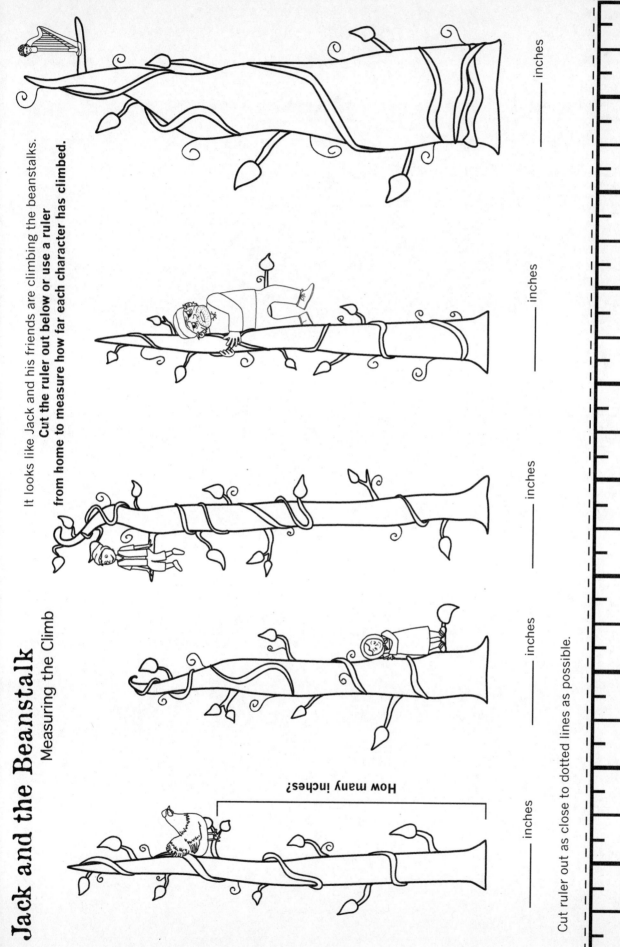

How many inches?

_____ inches

_____ inches

_____ inches

_____ inches

_____ inches

Cut ruler out as close to dotted lines as possible.

1 2 3 4 5 6 7 8 9

Jack and the Beanstalk
Measuring Beanstalks 2

More magic beans have sprouted!
Use a ruler from home or a ruler from the first
Measuring Beanstalks sheet to measure each beanstalk.

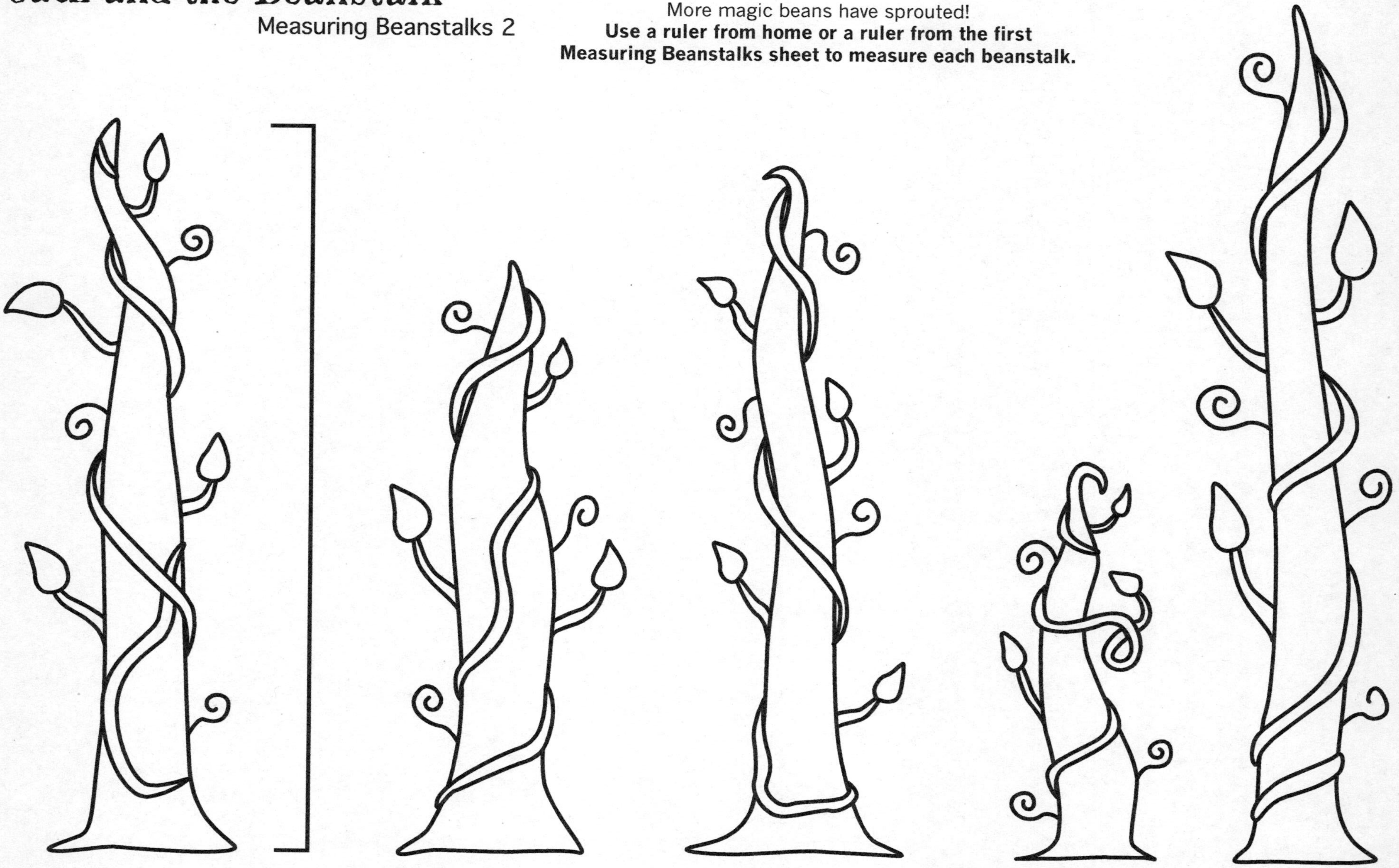

——— inches

——— inches

——— inches

——— inches

——— inches

111

Jack and the Beanstalk
Make Your Own Mini-Book Page 1

Create your own mini-book by illustrating it yourself!

1

Jack traded his cow for magic beans that grew into a beanstalk.

3

And saw a Giant that yelled, "Fee Fi Fo Fum!"

8

But Jack makes it home safely.

6

And a harp that played by itself.

fold

cut

Jack and the Beanstalk
Make Your Own Mini-Book Page 2

The Giant was angry and chased Jack.

7

And a hen that laid golden eggs.

5

Jack climbed the beanstalk.

2

Jack took gold coins from the Giant.

4

fold

cut

Jack and the Beanstalk
Sequencing Events

Oh no! This story is mixed up. Cut the pictures out and arrange them in the correct order.

You can add life to the pictures by coloring them or telling your own version of Jack and the Beanstalk.

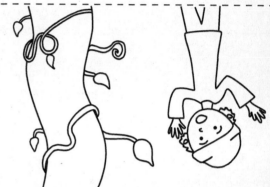

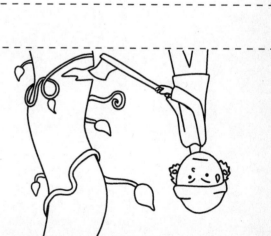

Add It Up! *with Jack*

Help Jack by solving the
word problems below.

1. Jack's hen lays **6** eggs on Monday, **3** eggs on Wednesday
   and **7** eggs on Saturday. How many eggs did Jack's hen
   lay?

   _____

2. The beanstalk had **7** leaves. The next day it grew **8** new
   leaves. How many leaves did the beanstalk have?

   _____

3. Jack is watching clouds float in the sky. He sees **4** puffy
   clouds over his house, **11** clouds around the beanstalk, and
   3 clouds in the distance. How many clouds did Jack see?

   _____

4. Jack buys **20** more magic beans from the old man. A few
   days later, **14** beans have sprouted up. How many beans
   have not sprouted up yet?

   _____

5. The magical harp knows **18** songs. Jack teaches the harp
   7 new songs but the harp can only remember **5** of them.
   How many songs does the harp know?

   _____

Irregular Measurements

Mr. and Mrs. Giant must have a kitchen to match their larger than life size.

To find out how large, answer the questions on the next page and use the footsteps to make the measurements.

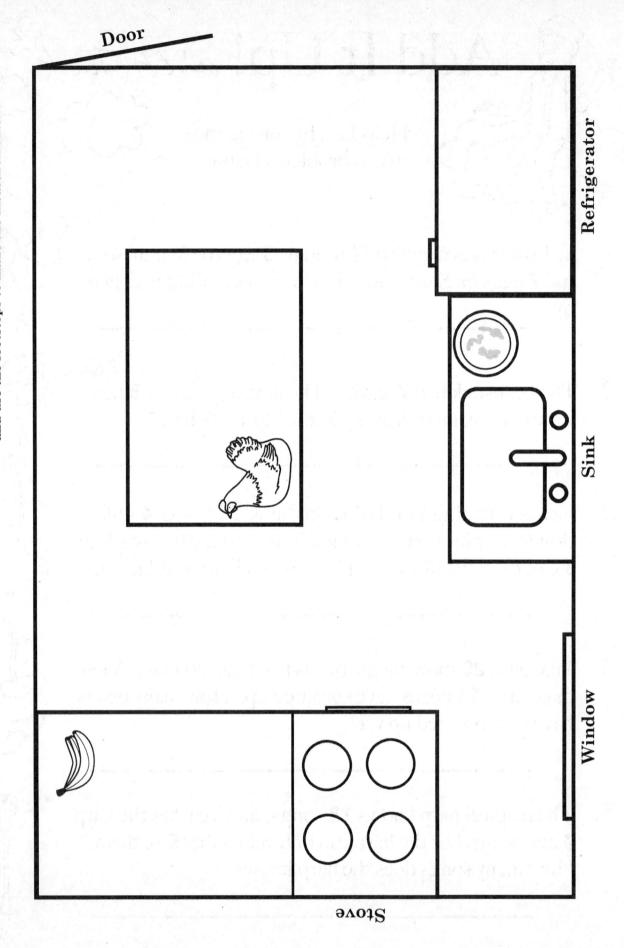

Door

Refrigerator

Sink

Window

Stove

Irregular Measurements

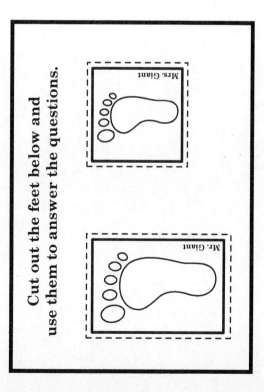

Cut out the feet below and
use them to answer the questions.

Mr. Giant

Mrs. Giant

How Large?

1. Using Mrs. Giant's footprint, how long is the table?

2. Using Mr. Giant's footprint, how long is the table?

3. Using Mrs. Giant's footprint, how wide is the room?

4. Using Mr. Giant's footprint, how long is the room?

How Many Steps?

1. Starting at the door, about how many steps would
   Mrs. Giant take to wash the dirty dish?

2. Starting at the door, about how many steps would
   Mrs. Giant take to cook something on the stove?

3. Starting at the door, about how many steps would
   Mrs. Giant take to walk around the table back to the door?

4. Starting at the door, about how many steps would
   Mrs. Giant take to open the window?

5. Starting at the door, about how many steps would
   Mr. Giant take to eat a banana?

6. Starting at the door, about how many steps would
   Mr. Giant take to walk around the table to the chicken?

7. Starting at the door, about how many steps would
   Mr. Giant take to get eggs from the refrigerator?

8. Starting at the door, about how many steps would
   Mr. Giant take to open the window?

Great job!

_____

is an Education.com reading superstar